RECORDED VERSIONS
GUITAR

AUTHENTIC TRANSCRIPTIONS
WITH NOTES AND TABLATURE

Transcribed by JESSE GRESS

the Beatles RUBBER SOUL

D1616699

ISBN 0-7935-3162-4

HAL•LEONARD™
CORPORATION
7777 W. BLUEMOUND RD. P.O. BOX 13819 MILWAUKEE, WI 53213

Drive My Car

Words and Music by John Lennon and Paul McCartney

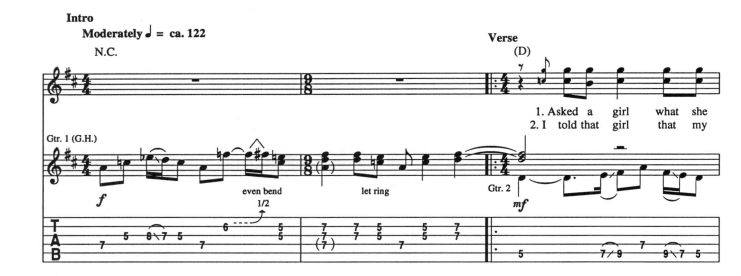

Intro

Moderately ♩ = ca. 122

N.C.

Verse (D)

Gtr. 1 (G.H.)

even bend 1/2

let ring

Gtr. 2

1. Asked a girl what she
2. I told that girl that my

(G)

want-ed to be,
pros-pects were good,

(D)

and she said, "Ba-by, can't you see?
and she said, "Ba-by, it's un-der-stood.

(G)

Gtr. 1 tacet

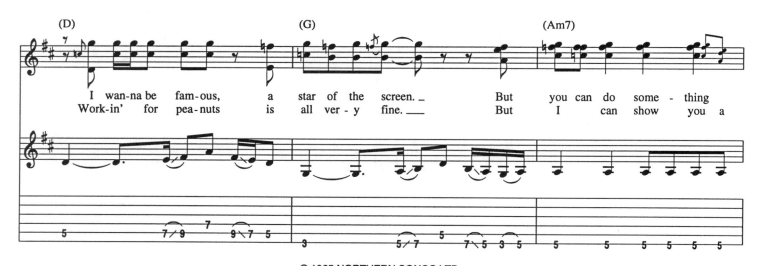

(D)

I wan-na be fam-ous, a star of the screen.
Work-in' for pea-nuts is all ver-y fine.

(G)

(Am7)

But you can do some-thing
But I can show you a

Guitar Solo
(P.McC.)

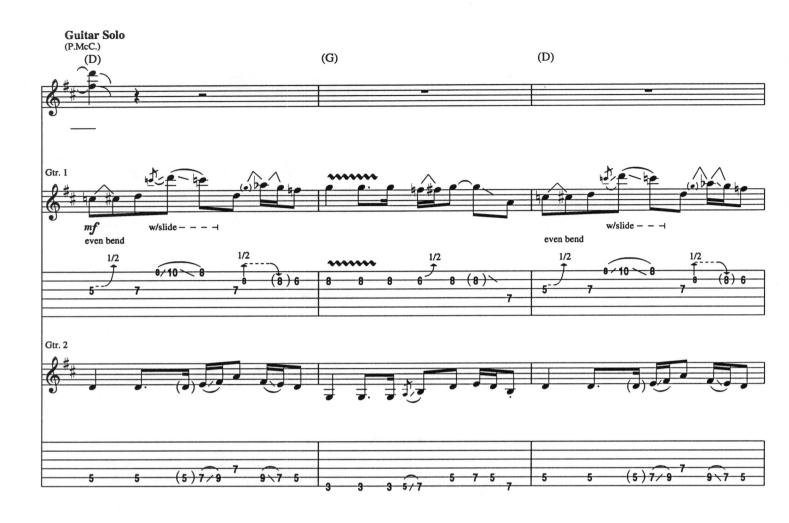

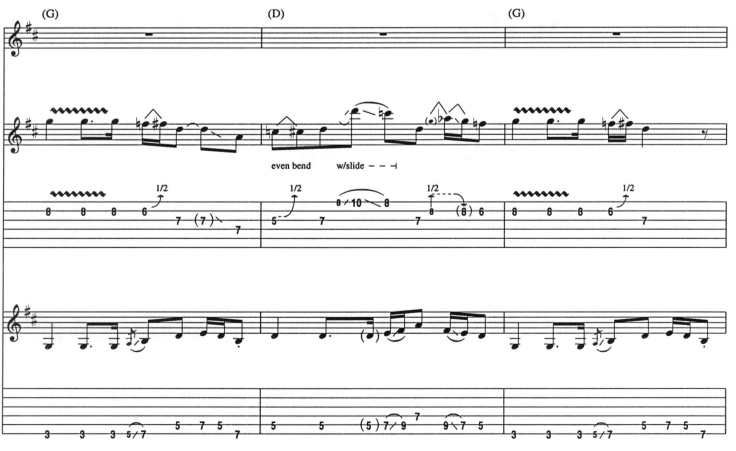

4

5

Verse

3. I told that girl I could start right a - way, ___

and she said, "Lis-ten babe, ___ I got some-thin' to say. ___ I got no car an' it's

break-in' my heart, ___ but I found a driv - er, and that's a start. ___

D.S. al Coda

Coda

Beep, beep, mm - beep, beep, yeah! ___

Norwegian Wood
(This Bird Has Flown)

Words and Music by John Lennon and Paul McCartney

† Gtr. 2 and 12- str. Acous. Gtr. capoed at 2nd fret.
  Notes tabbed at 2nd fret played as open strings.

MCA music publishing

room, is - n't it good? Nor - we - gian wood. She

asked me to stay and she told me to sit an - y - where.

Bridge

10

So I looked a - round and I no - ticed there was - n't a chair.

2. I sat on a rug bid - ing my time, drink - ing her

Em

F#m7

B

End Rhy. Fig. 2

End Rhy. Fig. 2

Let ring - - - - -

Verse
* w/Rhy. Fig. 1

E

Dadd9

Sitar arr. for gtr.

* Rhy. Fig. 1 includes Acous. Gtr. 1 and 12-str. Accous.

11

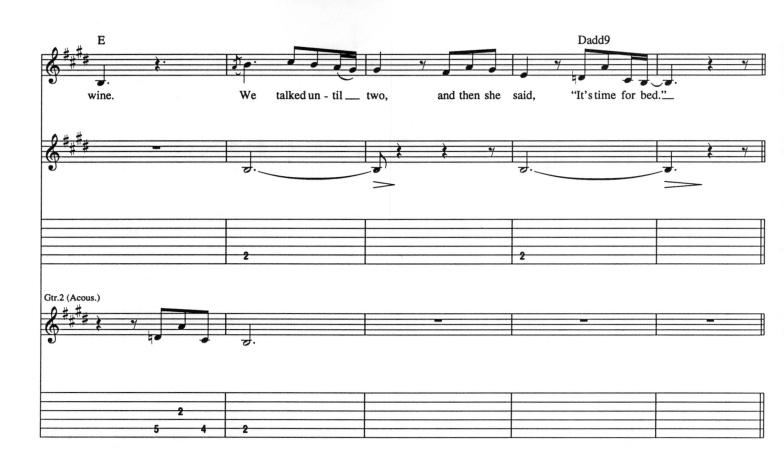

wine. We talked un - til ___ two, and then she said, "It's time for bed."

Instrumental

Bridge
* w/Rhy. Fig. 2

told me she worked in the morn - ing and start - ed to laugh. ___

* Rhy. Fig. 2 includes acous. gtr. 1
and 12-str. acous.

told her I did-n't and crawled off to sleep in the bath. ___

Verse
**w/Rhy. Fig. 1

3. And when I a - woke I was a - lone, ___ this bird had

Sitar arr. for gtr.

** Rhy. Fig. 1 includes acous. gtr. 1 and 12-str. acous.

flown.   So   I   lit a fire.   Is - n't it good?   Nor-we-gian wood.

You Won't See Me

Words and Music by John Lennon and Paul McCartney

MCA music publishing

Nowhere Man

Words and Music by John Lennon and Paul McCartney

Moderately ♩ = ca 122

*Acous. Gtr. capoed at 2nd fret.

Notes tabbed at 2nd fret played as open strings

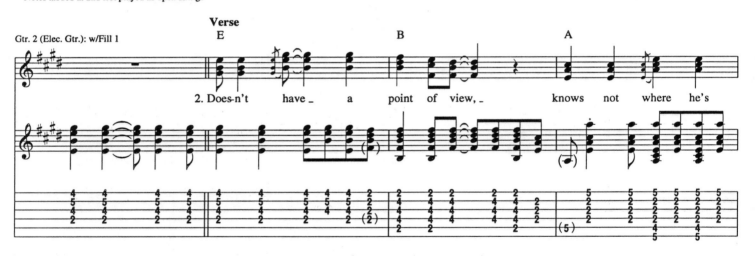

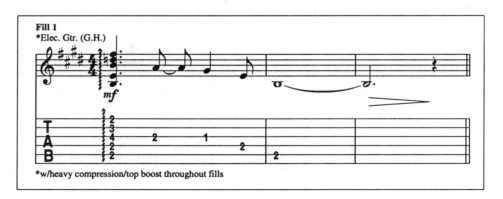

*w/heavy compression/top boost throughout fills

MCA music publishing

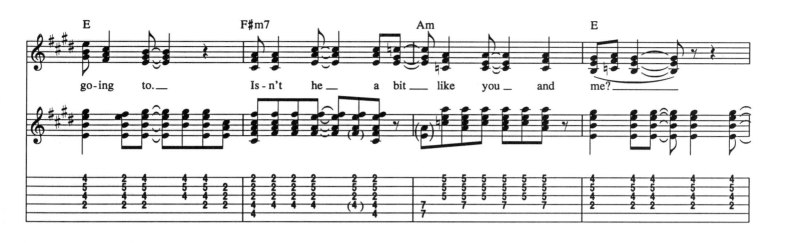

go-ing to.___ Is-n't he __ a bit __ like __ you __ and me?_____

%S Bridge

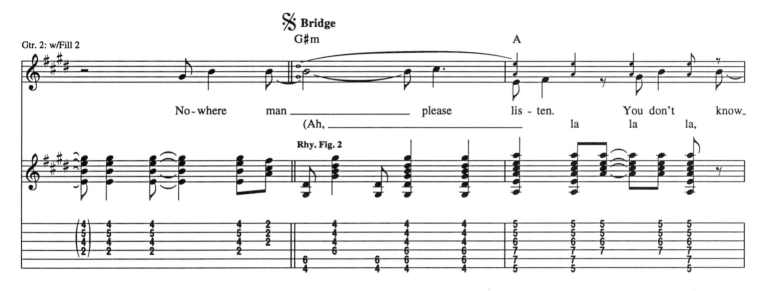

Gtr. 2: w/Fill 2

G#m   A

No-where man _____ please lis - ten.   You don't   know_
(Ah, _____   la   la   la,

Rhy. Fig. 2

G#m   A   G#m

_____   No - where __ man, __   the
ah, _____ miss-ing.   la   la   la,   ah, _____
what __ you're

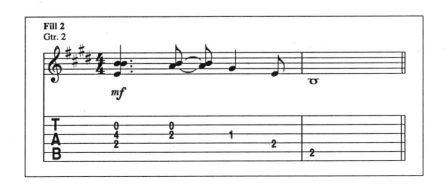

Fill 2
Gtr. 2

mf

21

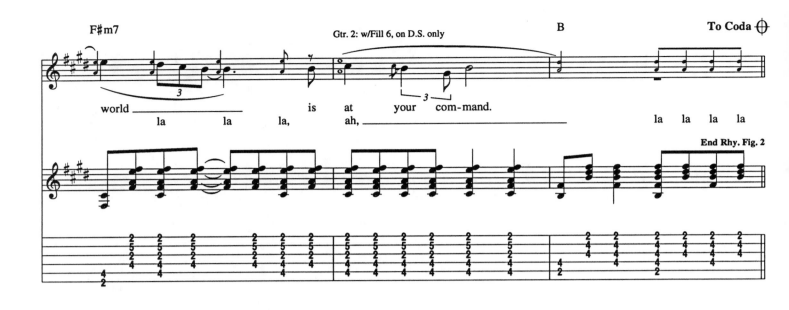

world _____ _____ is at your com-mand.
la la la la, ah, _____ la la la la

la.)

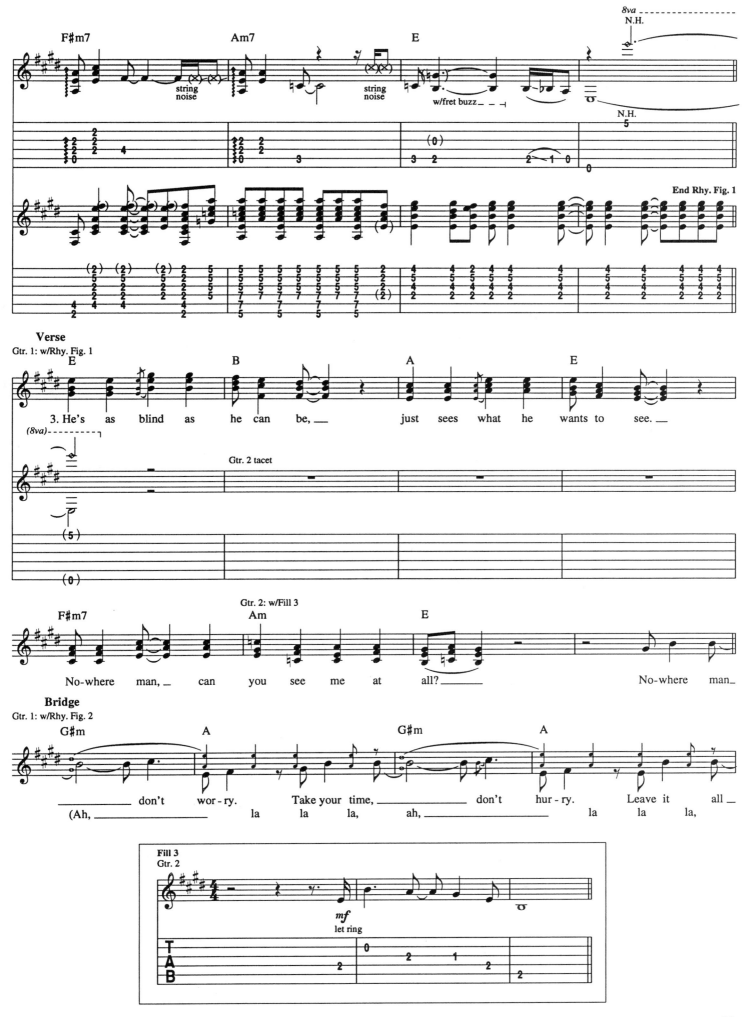

'til some-bod-y else ___ lends ___ you a hand. ___
ah, _____ la la la, ah, _____ la la la la.)

Verse
Gtr. 1: w/Rhy. Fig. 1

4. Does-n't have a point of view, ___ knows not where he's go-ing to. ___

Gtr. 2: w/Fill 5

D.S. al Coda

Is-n't he ___ a bit ___ like you ___ and me? ___ No-where man, ___

Coda
Verse
Gtr. 1: w/Rhy. Fig. 1

5. He's a re - al no - where ___ man, sit-ting in ___ his

no - where ___ land, mak-ing all ___ his no - where plans for no - bod - y.

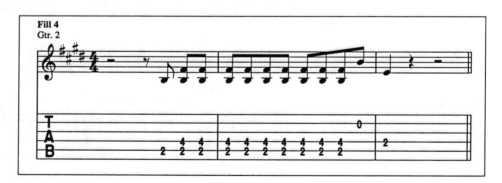

Fill 4
Gtr. 2

Fill 5
Gtr. 2

Think For Yourself

Words and Music by George Harrison

*Gtr. 1 capoed at 3rd fret.
Notes tabbed at 3rd fret played as open strings.

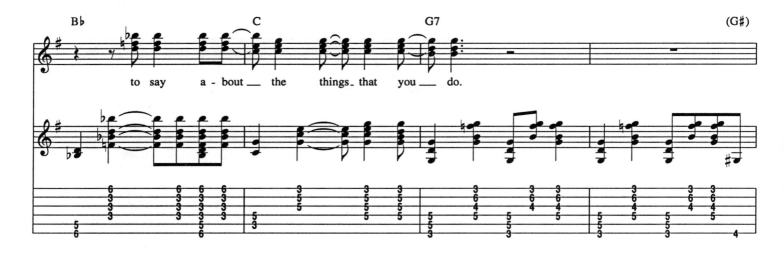

MCA music publishing

things that __ we can __ have if __ we close __ our eyes. __

End Rhy. Fig. 1

Do what you want to do, __ and go where you're go - ing to. __

Rhy. Fig. 2
Gtr. 1

Think for your-self, 'cause I __ won't be there_ with you. __

End Rhy. Fig. 2

Verse
Gtr. 1: w/Rhy. Fig. 1

2. I left __ you far __ be-hind, the ru-ins of __ the life __ that you __ had in mind.

And though_you still __ can't _ see, I know your mind's_ made up, __ you're gon-

Gtr. 1: w/Rhy. Fig. 2

na cause_ more_ mis - er - y. __ Do what you want to do, __ and go where you're go-ing to. __

Think for your-self, 'cause I __ won't be there_ with you. __

27

Verse

Gtr. 1: w/Rhy. Fig. 1

3. Al-though your mind's o - paque, try think-ing more if just for your own sake.

The fu-ture still looks good, and you've got time to rec-ti-fy all the things that

Gtr. 1: w/Rhy. Fig. 2

you should. Do what you want to do, and go where you're go-ing to.

Gtr. 1: w/Rhy. Fig. 2, 1st 6 measures

Think for your-self, 'cause I will be there with you. Do what you want to do,

and go where you're go-ing to. Think for your-self, 'cause I won't be there with you.

Think for your-self, 'cause

I won't be there with you.

The Word

Words and Music by John Lennon and Paul McCartney

Intro
Moderately ♩ = ca 126

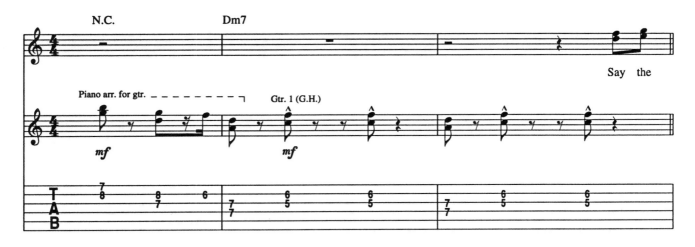

Say the

Verse

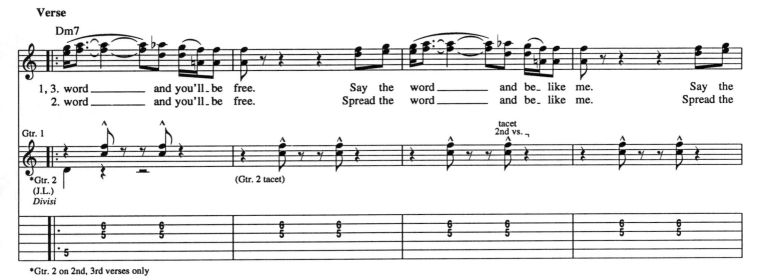

1, 3. word _____ and you'll_ be free. Say the word _____ and be_ like me. Say the

2. word _____ and you'll_ be free. Spread the word _____ and be_ like me. Spread the

*Gtr. 2 on 2nd, 3rd verses only

word _____ I'm think-in' of. Have you heard? _____ The word_ is "love." It's

word _____ I'm think-in' of. Have you heard? _____ The word_ is "love."

MCA music publishing

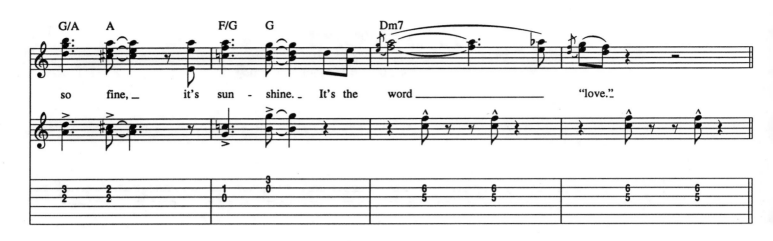

so fine, __ it's sun - shine. __ It's the word _____ "love."

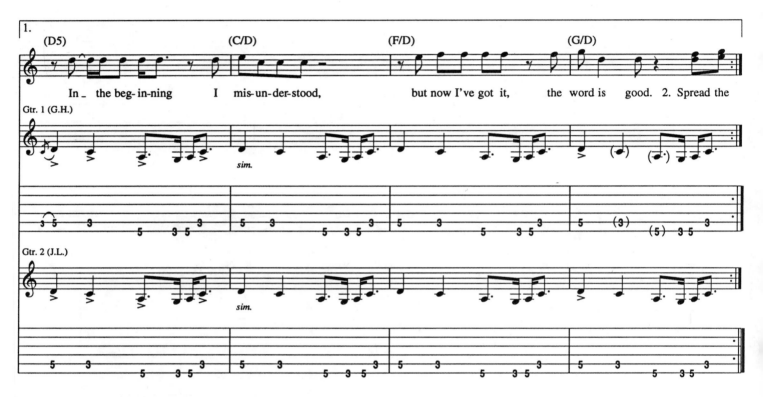

1.

In __ the beg-in-ning I mis-un-der-stood, but now I've got it, the word is good. 2. Spread the

Gtr. 1 (G.H.)

Gtr. 2 (J.L.)

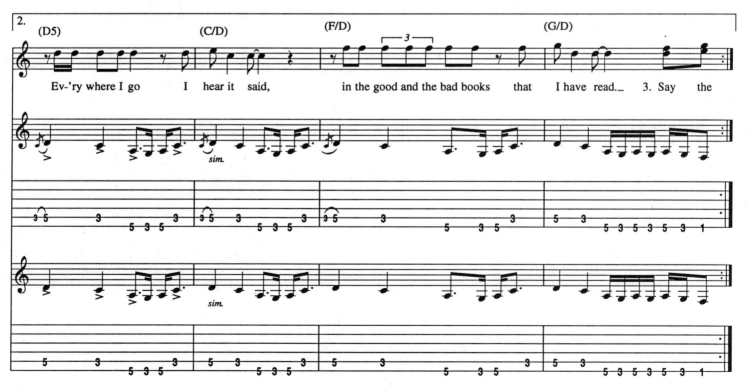

2.

Ev-'ry where I go I hear it said, in the good and the bad books that I have read. __ 3. Say the

Harmonium Solo

Verse

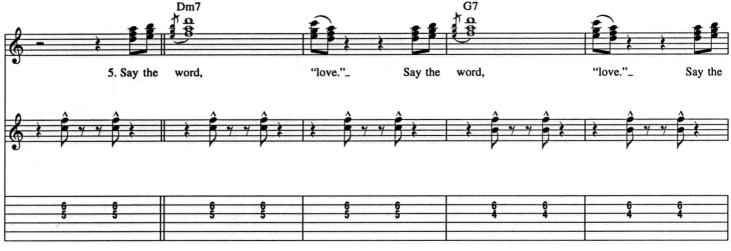

5. Say the word, "love."_ Say the word, "love."_ Say the

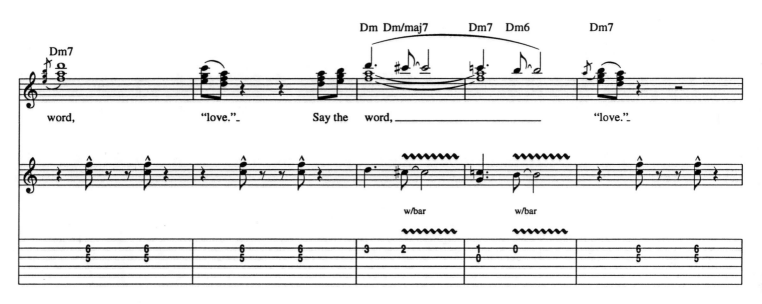

word, "love."_ Say the word,_____ "love."

w/bar   w/bar

Harmonium Solo

Begin Fade   *Fade out*

Michelle

Words and Music by John Lennon and Paul McCartney

MCA music publishing

34

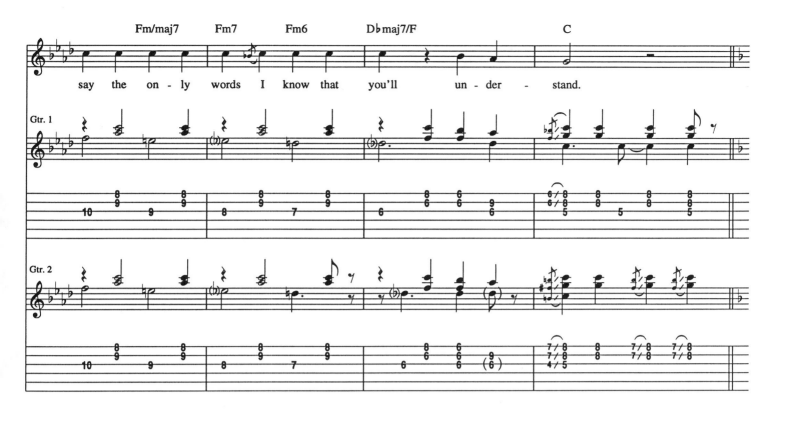

say the on - ly words I know that you'll un - der - stand.

Gtr. 1

Gtr. 2

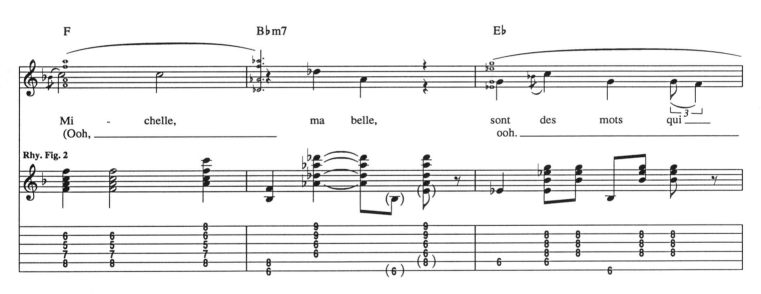

Mi - chelle, ma belle, sont des mots qui
(Ooh, _____ ooh. _____

Rhy. Fig. 2

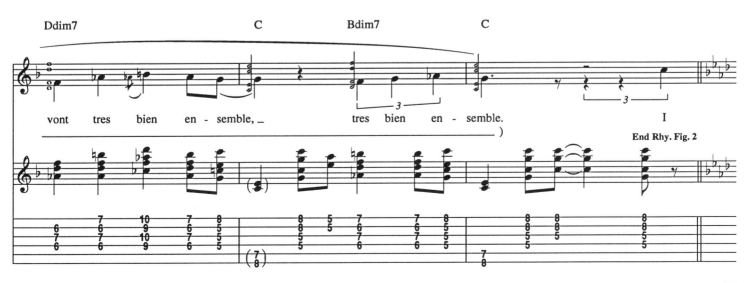

vont tres bien en - semble, _ tres bien en - semble.
)

End Rhy. Fig. 2

I

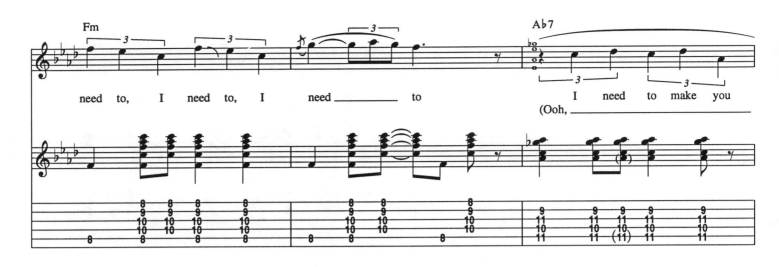

need to, I need to, I   need _____ to   I need to make you
                                                                          (Ooh, _____

        see.   Oh, what you   mean to ___ me. ___   Un -
        ___   Ooh. _____)

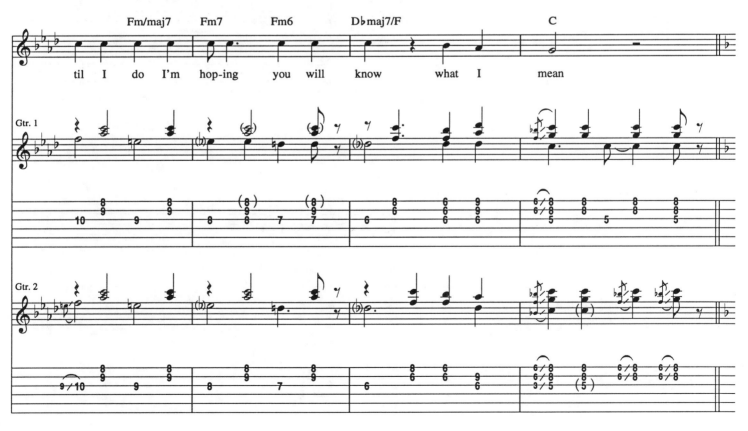

til I   do I'm hop-ing   you   will   know   what   I   mean

What Goes On

Words and Music by John Lennon, Paul McCartney and Richard Starkey

MCA music publishing

What goes on _____ in your mind?_ You are tear-

ing me a-part ___ when you treat_

me so un - kind. ___ What goes on ___

To Coda

in your mind? ___

1. The

42

like you to lie.   Tell me why.   What goes on

in your heart?   What goes on

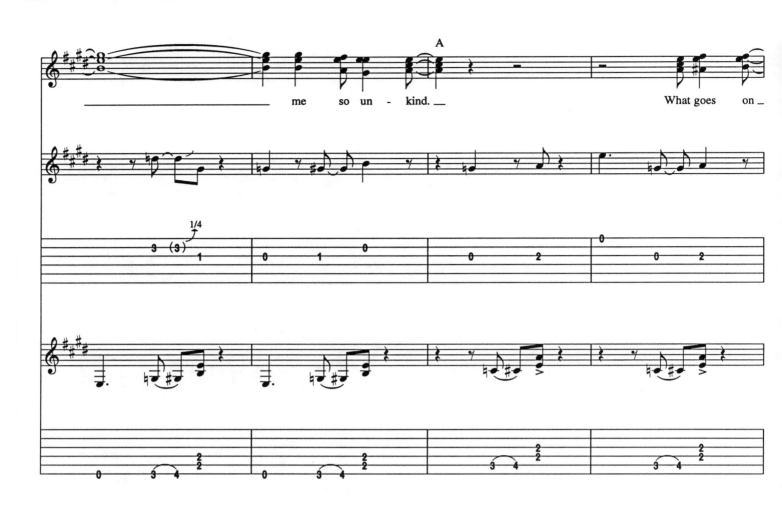

me   so   un - kind. ___   What goes   on _

_____   in your   mind? _   2. I

Verse

Gtr. 2: w/Rhy. Fig. 1

met you in ____ the morn - ing wait - ing for the tides ____ of time.__

(Ooh, ____

____ But now the tides ____ are turn - ing, I ____ can

ooh, ____

see that I was blind. ____ It's so eas - y for a girl ____

ooh. ____

____ like you to lie ____)

Tell me why. __

What goes on _____ in your heart?

let ring

Guitar Solo

let ring throughout solo

⊕ *Coda*

(in your mind, __

in your mind. __)

Girl

Words and Music by John Lennon and Paul McCartney

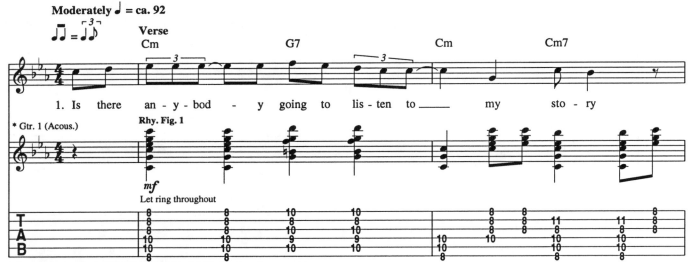

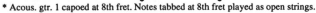

* Acous. gtr. 1 capoed at 8th fret. Notes tabbed at 8th fret played as open strings.

MCA music publishing

man must break his back to earn his day of lei- sure? Will she still be - lieve. it when he's dead? Ah, __

Chorus

girl, _____ fffff, _____ girl, ____ girl. ____

(breathe in)

Interlude

Gtr. 3 (Acous. 12-str.)

Gtr. 2 (Acous.)

Gtr. 1 (Acous.)

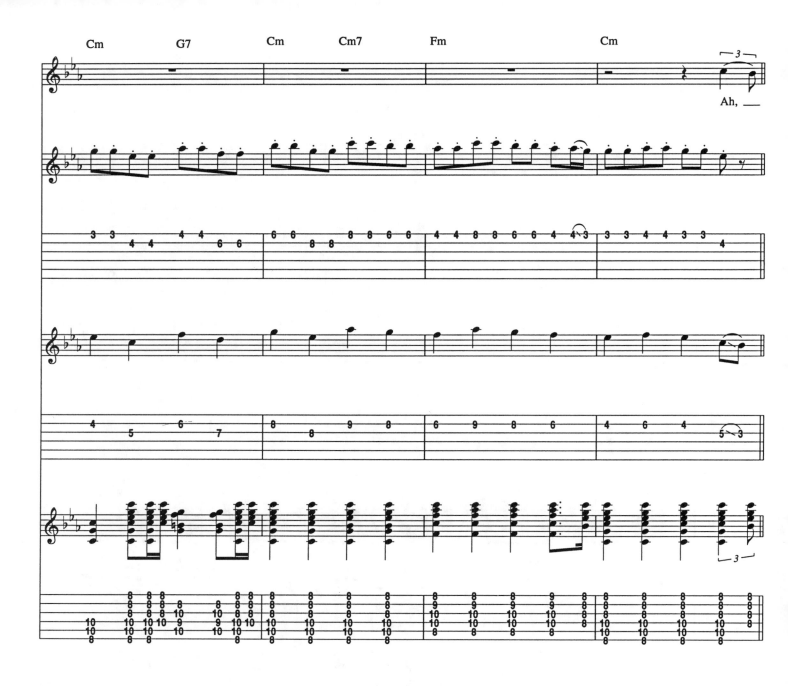

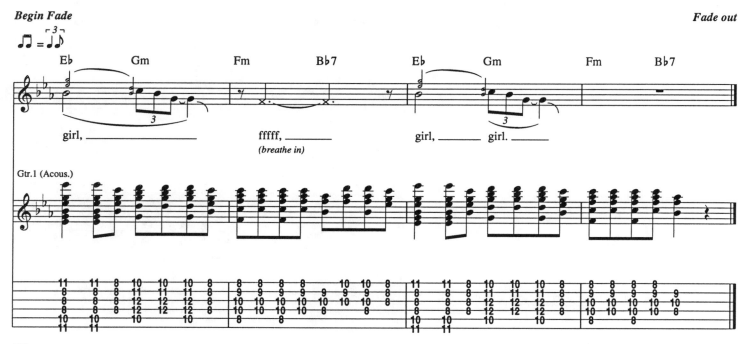

I'm Looking Through You

Words and Music by John Lennon and Paul McCartney

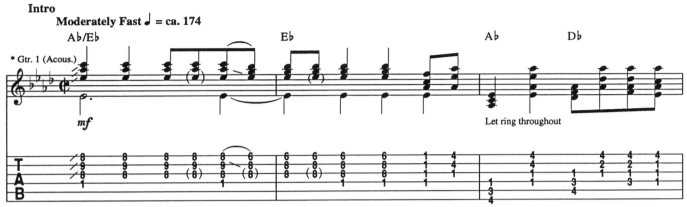

* Acous. gtr. capoed at 1st fret throughout.
Notes tabbed at 1st fret are played as open strings.

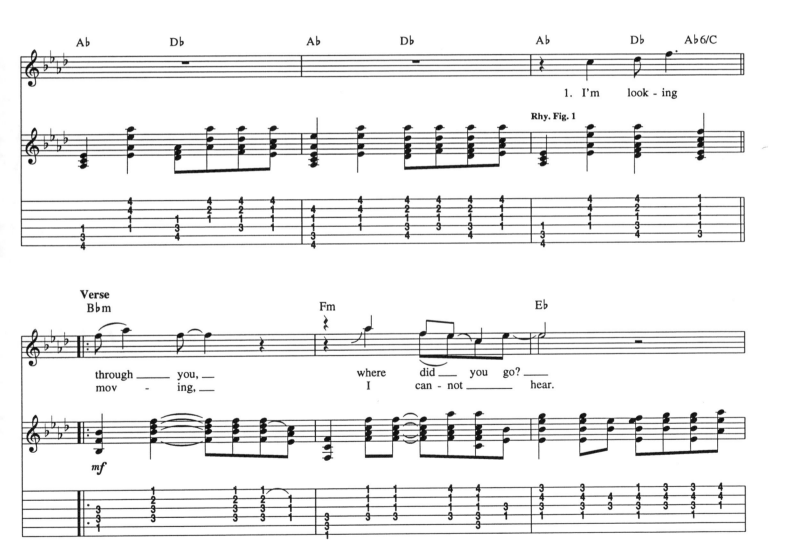

MCA music publishing

I thought I knew ___ you, ___   what did I ___ know?___
Your voice is sooth - ing, ___   but the words are - n't ___

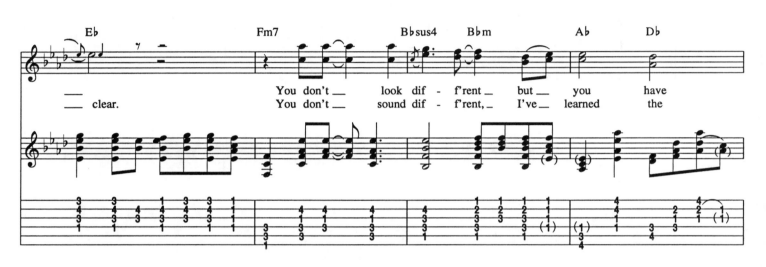

___ clear.
___ clear. You don't ___ look dif - f'rent ___ but ___ you have
___ clear. You don't ___ sound dif - f'rent, I've learned the

Gtr. 2: w/Fill 1, 2nd time only

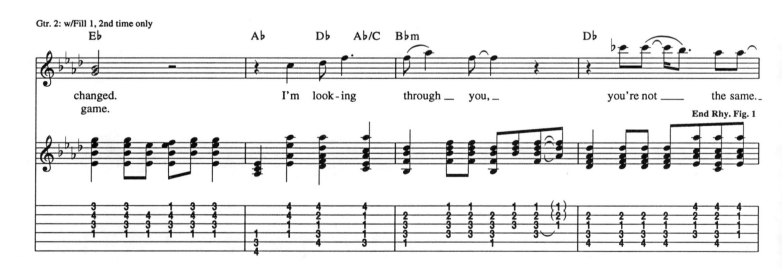

changed.   I'm look - ing through ___ you, ___   you're not ___ the same.
game.

End Rhy. Fig. 1

Fill 1
Gtr. 2 (Elec.), capo I

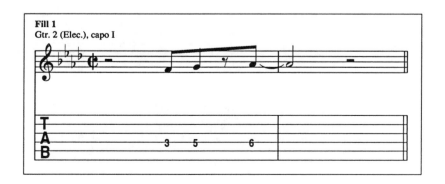

58

2. You're lips   are

* Gtr. 2 (Elec.)

f
(w/fuzz)

* Elec. gtr. also capoed at 1st fret. Notes tabbed at 1st fret played as open strings.

Gtr. 1 (Acous.)

f

Gtr. 2 (Elec.)

f
(w/fuzz)

Gtr. 1 (Acous.)

f

Bridge

Why, _____ tell me why _ did you _ not treat me right? _

* Elec. gtr. notated to right of / in TAB.

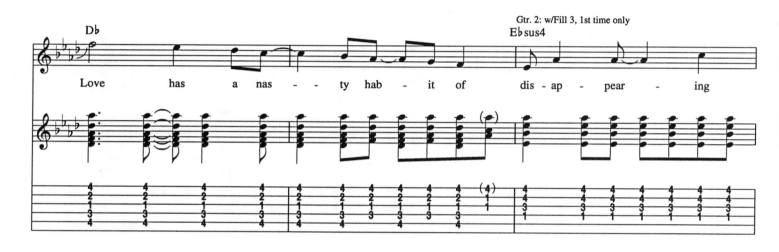

Love has a nas - - ty hab - it of dis - ap - pear - ing

Verse
Gtr. 1: w/Rhy. Fig. 1

ov - er - night. ___

3. You're think - ing of ___ me ___ the same _ old _
4. I'm look - ing through _ you, _ where did you go?.

Fill 2
* Gtr.2 (Elec.)

* Capo at 1st fret.

Fill 3
* Gtr.2 (Elec.)

* Capo at 1st fret.

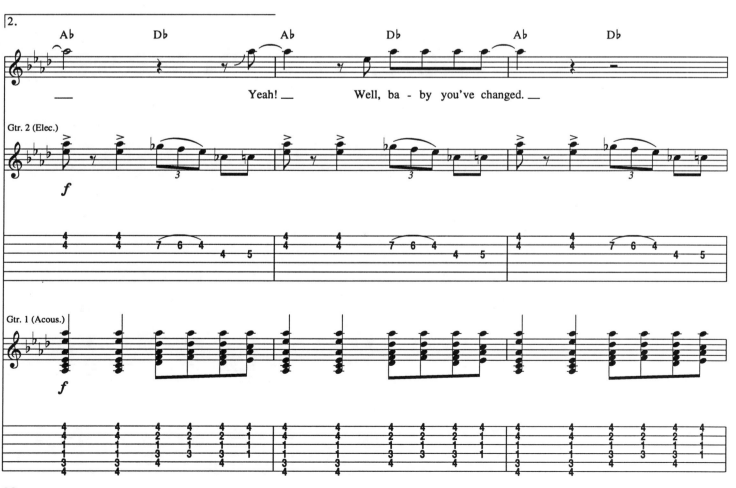

In My Life

Words and Music by John Lennon and Paul McCartney

MCA music publishing

Piano solo
arr. for 2 guitars

Wait

Words and Music by John Lennon and Paul McCartney

MCA music publishing

If I Needed Someone

Words and Music by George Harrison

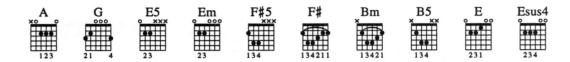

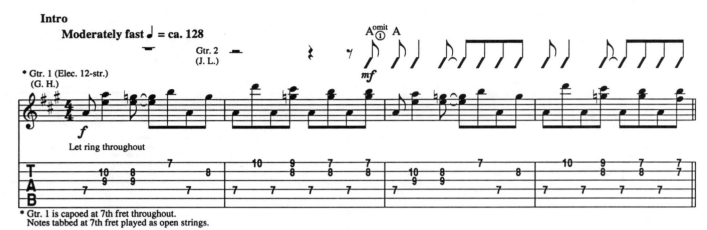

Intro

Moderately fast ♩ = ca. 128

* Gtr. 1 (Elec. 12-str.)
(G. H.)

Gtr. 2 (J. L.)

Let ring throughout

* Gtr. 1 is capoed at 7th fret throughout.
Notes tabbed at 7th fret played as open strings.

Verse

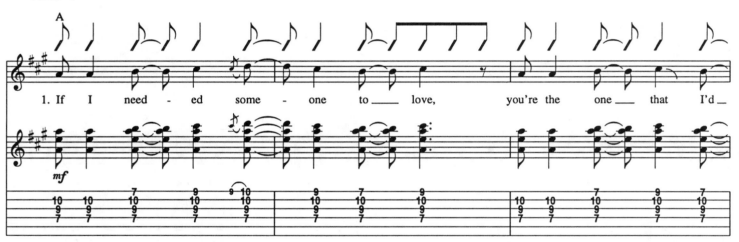

1. If I need-ed some-one to ___ love, you're the one ___ that I'd ___ be think-ing ___ of, ___ if I need-ed some-

MCA music publishing

77

Interlude

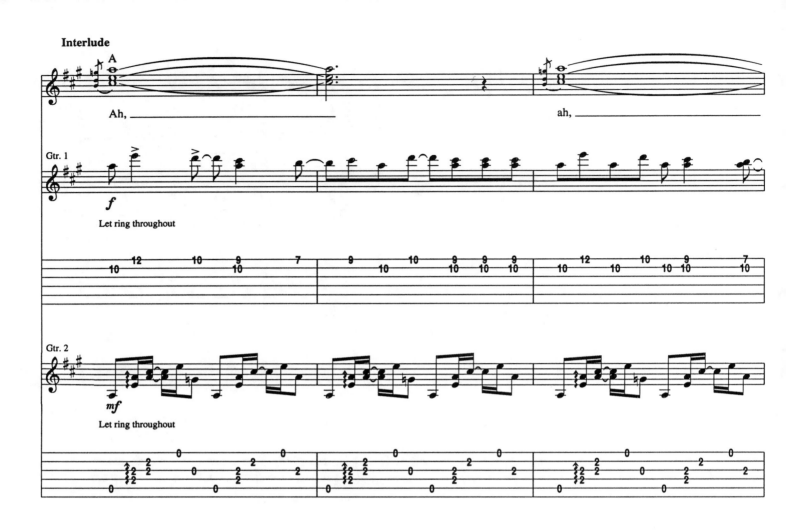

Ah, _____   ah, _____

Gtr. 1

f

Let ring throughout

Gtr. 2

mf

Let ring throughout

— ___   ah, _____

mp   *f*

Run For Your Life

Words and Music by John Lennon and Paul McCartney

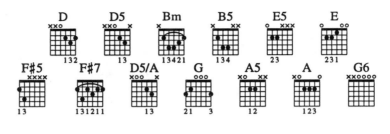

MCA music publishing

To Coda ⊕

Lyrics:
You bet-ter run for your life if you can, __ lit-tle girl. __ Hide your head __ in the sand __

__ lit - tle girl. __ Catch you with an-oth-er man __ that's the end __ ah, lit-tle

girl.

2. Well, you
4. I'd

Elec. Gtr. 1

Elec. Gtr. 2

Elec. Gtr. 3

84

NOTATION LEGEND